Religious discrimination

a Christian response

Religious discrimination

a Christian response

A discussion document from the
Churches' Commission for Inter Faith Relations

CHURCHES TOGETHER
IN BRITAIN AND IRELAND

Churches Together in Britain and Ireland
Inter-Church House, 35–41 Lower Marsh
London SE1 7SA
Tel: +44 (0)20 7523 2121; Fax: +44 (0)20 7928 0010
info@ctbi.org.uk or (team)@ctbi.org.uk
www.ctbi.org.uk

Registered charity number 259688
ISBN: 0 85169 259 1

Published 2001 by Churches Together in Britain and Ireland

Produced by Church House Publishing

Further copies available from: CTBI Publications, 31 Great Smith Street,
London SW1P 3BN Tel: +44 (0)20 7898 1300; Fax: +44 (0)20 7898 1305;
orders@ctbi.org.uk   www.chbookshop.co.uk

Cover design by Visible Edge

Typeset in 10 on 12pt Sabon by Vitaset, Paddock Wood, Kent TN12 6JR

Printed in England by Halstan & Co. Ltd, Amersham, Bucks

Contents

Foreword

by The Revd Baroness Richardson of Calow

What gives an individual or a community their identity? How should that identity be publicly recognized and, where necessary, protected? How can we create a context of trust in which people of different faiths feel able to join together in public and civic life? These are problems of ever-growing importance and urgency as we move into a new millennium. All our four nations are now places where Christians of different traditions live and work alongside Baha'is, Buddhists, Hindus, Jains, Jews, Muslims, Sikhs, Zoroastrians and other people of faith, as well as those of no religion.

This report focuses on Christian attitudes in an area where questions of religious identity and of inter faith relations come together in a very practical way. The reality of religious discrimination fundamentally threatens our common quest for social cohesion. It challenges us to find ways of living creatively with difference at the deepest levels of our lives. It is something that Christians must take seriously, not only because of the possible effects of any legislation on the Churches' own organization, but also because we have a concern for the common good.

I commend this short report to all who wish to explore further what contribution Christians might have to make in this area. It offers an overall framework that I believe will prove very helpful in moving the discussion forward. On many important points, it traces an emerging agreement among Christians of different traditions. On other questions, it is evident that no consensus yet exists, and debate needs to continue among and within the Churches. However complex and sensitive the ramifications, we need to recognize that these are issues of such importance that to remain silent could in effect be to adopt a position by default.

Kathleen Richardson
(Moderator, Churches' Commission for Inter Faith Relations)

Explanatory notes

This report

In November 1999, the Church Representatives' Meeting of Churches Together in Britain and Ireland (CTBI) discussed Christian attitudes to the possibility of legislation regarding religious discrimination. They concluded that the Churches:

- welcome the fact that the UK Government will be acting only in the light of careful research through the University of Derby Research Project (a study commissioned by the Home Office into the extent and nature of religious discrimination in England and Wales);

- affirm on the basis of a commitment to religious liberty and social justice their repudiation in principle of religious discrimination;

- would welcome the UK Government bringing forward proposals for legislation if a problem is shown to exist;

- recognize that this is a complex area, and that great care would be needed in framing any such legislation to ensure that it was workable, that it took account of the needs of Churches and other faith communities to organize their own lives with integrity, that it could deal successfully with the question of what constituted religion, and did not prove divisive;

- therefore believe that careful consultation with all Churches and faith communities would be needed in the framing of any legislation; and

- encourage the Churches' Commission for Inter Faith Relations (CCIFR) to continue consultations on this issue.

This short report from CCIFR is offered in response to that invitation. It does not claim to express with authority the views of the member Churches of CTBI, but is offered as a resource to Christians wishing to engage with these important yet complex issues more deeply. It does, however, stand within the broad approach to this question established by CTBI in their 1999 statement.

The Churches' Commission for Inter Faith Relations (CCIFR)

CCIFR is one of the commissions of Churches Together in Britain and Ireland, and includes representatives of 15 member bodies of CTBI. Its terms of reference are:

– to enable the Churches to engage effectively in relations and dialogue with other faith communities in Britain and Ireland;

– to be a point of reference in the Churches for faith-to-faith encounter;

– to facilitate a network of information and experience among Christians about inter faith relations;

– to enable critical reflection on the religiously and socially plural society of these islands.

CCIFR seeks to fulfil these aims by:

• advising church leaders on inter faith issues

• monitoring inter faith relations nationally

• nurturing links between Christians working in this field

• pooling the theological resources of the Churches for ministry and witness in this area

• producing appropriate written or other material to help the Churches.

CCIFR is affiliated on behalf of CTBI to the Inter Faith Network for the United Kingdom, which provides a national forum for people from the main faith communities to meet, discuss and share.

Michael Ipgrave
(Secretary, Churches' Commission for Inter Faith Relations)

Asking some questions

There is a growing perception among many people that discrimination on the grounds of religion or belief is a serious problem, repeatedly experienced in the societies of our islands. Evidence for these claims in England and Wales has been gathered in a research study commissioned by the Home Office from the University of Derby. The study's brief was to examine the scale and patterns of religious discrimination, to explore its overlap with racial discrimination, and to suggest policy options for dealing with the problem. The authors' cautious conclusion was as follows:

> Ignorance and indifference towards religion were of widespread concern amongst research participants from all faith groups ... Ignorance and indifference do not in themselves constitute discrimination, but in organisational settings they can contribute towards an environment in which 'unwitting' and institutional discrimination are able to thrive.[1]

Moreover, members of certain religious groups reported that they were experiencing religious discrimination to a disproportionately high degree.[2]

At the same time, the legal situation has developed significantly in two respects. The Human Rights Act 1998 has meant that since October 2000 the European Convention on Human Rights (ECHR) has been incorporated into UK law. A European Union directive, to be implemented in EU member states by December 2003, identifies 'religion or belief' as one of the grounds of discrimination to be eliminated in providing a framework for equal treatment in employment. Together, these two developments point to an increased public focus in all our nations on ways of tackling religious discrimination, including legislative methods.[3]

This is an important issue for the Christian Churches in Britain and Ireland for several reasons. A commitment to justice means that we need to take seriously people's claims to be victims of any form of discrimination. A theological understanding of what it means to be human recognizes the central place that religion and belief occupy in personal and communal

1

identity. Churches and Christian organizations are well placed to develop practical responses to combat religious discrimination. Legislation in this area will relate closely to many areas of the Churches' life and work.

Facing these complex and sensitive issues, Christians will look for guidance from the Churches. In our experience, ten of the most frequently asked questions are these:

1. Why is religious discrimination a serious problem?

2. Why should Christians be concerned about religious discrimination?

3. Should not people of other faiths fit in when they come to live in Christian countries like ours?

4. How can Christians treat people of other faiths equally if we believe that our religion is better than theirs?

5. Why should we protect the rights of minority faiths here when Christians are suffering overseas?

6. Does not the law already provide protection against religious discrimination?

7. Might not a law against religious discrimination cause more problems than it solves?

8. Would a law against religious discrimination mean that Christian organizations could no longer insist on appointing only Christians to such posts as ministers or teachers?

9. Would a law against religious discrimination mean that people could not criticize one another's beliefs?

10. Would not a law against religious discrimination unfairly favour people of other faiths?

This short report is offered as a resource for Christians wishing to probe a little further into the issues raised by questions such as these. We offer our reflections in four areas, as follows. In Chapter 1 we discuss what is meant by speaking of 'religious discrimination'. In Chapter 2 we look at the historical and theological background to the contemporary Christian affirmation of religious freedom, on the basis of which religious discrimination is repudiated. In Chapter 3 we outline some of the practical ways in which Churches can be involved in fighting against religious discrimination. In Chapter 4 we consider from a Christian perspective some of the questions raised by legislation in this area. We then come back to the ten questions above, offering on the basis of our arguments some points in response.

CHAPTER ONE

The meaning of religious discrimination

'Religious discrimination', as a shorthand expression for 'discrimination on the basis of religion or belief', involves two key terms: 'religion' (or 'belief'), and 'discrimination', and both words raise questions of interpretation. In this chapter, we look at each in turn, and then give examples of some practical situations relating to religious discrimination.

Religion

'Religion' has proved exceptionally elusive of definition in a number of different contexts. Legally, it has proved difficult to establish with any consistency the essential characteristics that qualify an organization or activity as religious.[1] In academic disciplines too there is no consensus over the meaning of the word. Some proposed definitions reflect the preconceptions of one particular type of religion in such a way as to exclude others. For example, reference to 'God' as an essential component in religion effectively excludes a faith such as Buddhism.[2] Others attempt to proceed by enumerating the various features actually found in religions in such a comprehensive way that the 'definition' becomes little more than a descriptive list.

From the standpoint of Christian theology also, the general concept of religion, like particular actual religions, has been understood in a wide variety of ways. Some theologians have condemned all forms of religion as illegitimate human substitutes for the gospel. Others have endorsed various religions as authentic vehicles of salvific life alongside the gospel. Between these two poles, many have sought criteria for distinguishing between different religious elements in the light of the gospel. These three approaches all involve theological judgements about the truth of religion in general or of religions in particular. Such judgements, though, should not be confused with the equally theological challenge of formulating a Christian basis for upholding religious freedom and opposing religious discrimination. Such a general principle could then be applied to the particular beliefs, practices and communities found in Britain and Ireland today that claim for themselves status as religions.

An approach like this, that builds pragmatically on a principled commitment to religious freedom, will extend beyond the generally recognized world faiths.[3] On the one hand, it will include lesser known traditions and new religious movements. On the other hand, it will also cover the convictions of atheists, humanists and others who repudiate any form of religion. To convey this extended meaning, the expression 'religion or belief' is frequently used in human rights documents. For example, Article 9 of the European Convention on Human Rights asserts the freedom to change or to manifest 'religion or belief', under the general heading of 'freedom of thought, conscience and religion'. It is also with discrimination on grounds of 'religion or belief' in employment or occupation that a newly adopted European Union directive deals. In commenting on Article 9 of the ECHR, the European Court has declared:

> It is, in its religious dimension, one of the most vital elements that go to make up the identity of believers and their conception of life, but it is also a precious asset for atheists, agnostics, sceptics and the unconcerned.[4]

Therefore, it is discrimination on this wider basis of 'religion or belief' with which this document is concerned. This will be our meaning when for convenience we use the shorter term 'religious discrimination'.[5]

Discrimination

The meaning of 'discrimination' also needs some clarification, and here help can be gained from comparison with the patterns of racial discrimination that have been the attention of far more academic and political interest to date. The University of Derby Research Project on Religious Discrimination suggests that there exists a range of behaviour and attitudes linked to unfair treatment of people, whether that be on the basis of religion or of race. They identify religious (or racial) discrimination within this range as follows:

- religious (or racial) prejudice

- religious (or racial) hatred

- religious (or racial) disadvantage

- religious (or racial) discrimination, direct or indirect

- 'institutional religionism' (corresponding to 'institutional racism').[6]

The last of the expressions in this list is a neologism formed on the analogy of a term highlighted by the report of the Stephen Lawrence Inquiry (1999). The Derby Project authors explain their coinage as follows:

> 'Institutional religionism' can be understood ... as the product of a combination of several factors into a mutually reinforcing environment and ethos. 'Institutional religionism' thus occurs in a context in which 'religious prejudice', 'direct' and 'indirect' religious discrimination combine in the collective failure of an organisation to provide an adequate and professional environment and service. Negligence and indifference often contribute to this failure.[7]

These various dimensions of unfair treatment will clearly feed into one another, and to some extent overlap. For example, prejudice creates the conditions where discrimination can flourish; hatred can be generated by intense prejudice; discrimination always implies some measure of disadvantage; so-called 'institutional religionism' arises from the embedding of discrimination within organizations. Moreover, religious discrimination in the strict sense can itself be either direct or indirect. The former involves 'the deliberate exclusion of people from opportunities or services on grounds related to their religious beliefs, identity or practice'. The latter refers to 'the exclusionary effects of historical decisions, contemporary structures or patterns of behaviour and organisation'.[8]

Given these close interconnections, an adequate Christian response to religious discrimination will have to be formulated at several levels. There may well be measures aimed specifically at discrimination, direct or indirect. For these to be effective, though, they will need to be complemented by education to combat prejudice, by the building of relationships to overcome hatred, by advocacy in the face of disadvantage, and by the development of good practice as a counter to the embedding of discrimination within organizations.

Examples

Some examples of religious discrimination are clear-cut. If a firm advertising job vacancies were to stipulate 'No Muslims need apply', this would be an unquestionable case of discrimination against people on the basis of their religion or belief. It would also, in all probability, be a straightforward manifestation of religious prejudice.

In other cases, the issues may be more complex, but the perception of religious discrimination can be equally strong. We give here some examples of various kinds of difficult situations of which we are aware. Not everybody would see all of these cases as necessarily instances of religious discrimination in the strict sense. However, each of them raises important questions about the meaning of religious discrimination, and about the best way to counter it.

1. A 15-year-old Muslim girl, of Indian ethnic background, wishes to spend a fortnight's work experience in a placement at the local branch of a national chain of stores, and her school arranges this for her. The management writes to the school that they are 'delighted to offer her this opportunity', as part of their 'commitment to ethnic and cultural diversity'. When the girl arrives for her first day of work experience, she is wearing a headscarf as she normally does. The manager asks her to remove this, as it is 'contrary to company dress code'. She refuses, and is sent home in tears.

    How far is it realistic or appropriate here to separate ethnic and cultural from religious factors? What can the company learn from this case about developing good practice?

2. An evangelical Christian mission working among the travelling community sets up, with the landlord's permission, a large tent in a field for a five-day Gospel convention. The mission team complain of substantial harassment from police officers patrolling at the entrance to the field: unexplained detentions of family members, aggressive questioning, repeated demands to the same people to produce documents every time they enter and leave the site. In the opinion of their leader (himself a Romany), they are experiencing this not only because they are gypsies, but also because they are Christians.

    How significant is it that the victims of harassment experience an overlap of racial and religious prejudice in this case? What positive role might local churches play in this situation?

3. A black-majority church in an inner-city neighbourhood wishes to set up a luncheon club for elderly people, and approaches the City Council to see what financial support might be available for this project. They are told by an official that they are not eligible for a grant, as the authority's policy is not to fund religious groups. The church leaders then point to the example of an elderly people's luncheon club held at a nearby gurdwara that receives grant support from the Council. The official replies that that club is eligible for funding under Council guidelines, because it provides a service for the Sikh community run by a Punjabi cultural organization.

    How far is it possible to distinguish between a group's religious and social activities in cases of this kind? How can a local authority establish funding guidelines that are consistent in the way they treat different religious and community groups?

4. When a local authority sets aside land on a new housing development to offer to religious groups at reduced rates, a Hindu group expresses a desire to build a temple and community centre there. A petition then begins to circulate among the newly arrived residents, objecting to the proposals and outlining concerns about parking, noise and possible disorder. When the organizers present the petition – that has several hundred signatures – to the local Council, they stress that they are not racist, but simply see no need for such a religious building in their neighbourhood. It is likely that about 25 per cent of the residents of the new development are of Hindu background – some of these are among the signatories of the petition.

   How important is it that this group should have public support to help them find a place to worship? What might a local inter faith group do to help in a situation like this?

5. A Church primary school with a reputation for academic excellence and high standards of discipline sees its main role as being to provide a good education for children from Christian families. The school operates, on a city-wide basis, an admissions policy that requires most applicants to supply a letter from their parish priest or another minister testifying to the family's active involvement in the worshipping life of a Christian church. The proportion of Asian pupils in the school is less than 5 per cent, while for the city as a whole it is more than 30 per cent. City clergy complain that frequently white families will suddenly appear at their churches, attend services for a few months, then never be seen again once they have received a letter for the school describing their active involvement in the church.

   How fair is the school's policy in the way that it treats families of different backgrounds? What can the school or the city churches do to remedy any unfairness, or any perception of unfairness?

6. An Asian office worker in a medium-sized firm finds in mid-life that, despite his previously rather secularized background, the practice of Islam has come to mean a great deal to him. He requests flexibility in his working hours on Friday afternoons, so that he can attend prayers in a local mosque. Although he explains that he is willing to make up the hours at other times, his manager's immediate response is a blunt refusal. When the employee persists, the manager warns him that his 'awkward' attitude will not further his career prospects.

   How reasonable is the firm being in the accommodation it is offering for the religious practices of its employee? What kind of training might help its staff to deal more creatively with this issue?

These examples point to the complexity of the issues involved, and the far-reaching implications of the questions raised. They are worth bearing in mind as a practical reference point in the following chapters, where we will explore some of the fundamental principles involved for the Churches in responding to religious discrimination.

CHAPTER TWO

Christians and religious freedom

Opposition to religious discrimination rests firmly on the principle of religious freedom. Although differing attitudes have been held through much of Christian history, this principle is generally recognized as fundamental in the Churches today. To discriminate against people because of their religious allegiance implies a curtailment of their right to freedom of religion. As such, religious discrimination must be unacceptable to Christians, because this is a right inherent in the created dignity of the human person. In this chapter, we explore the historical and theological background to this position, and also ask about the relation between a Christian understanding of religious freedom and other approaches.

Christian attitudes in history

It has to be recognized that the Churches as a whole have not always held a position in favour of general religious freedom. To understand the struggle through which the Christian affirmation of this principle has been reached, it is necessary to consider the counter-arguments used in the Churches in the past. Historically, we may distinguish between two kinds of justification for the enforcement of religious uniformity, or at least for discrimination against different religious communities. Though often found together, these two arguments rest on different premises: one essentially political in character, the other more strictly theological.

On the one hand, there has been the view that all the people of a given country should follow the same religion for the sake of social cohesion. In the European conflicts after the Reformation, this idea was sometimes justified by an appeal to the principle known as *cuius regio eius religio*,[1] that the ruler of a particular territory should be responsible for choosing the faith of all his or her subjects. This was a principle on which successive Tudor monarchs based their religious policies in the sixteenth century. The ecclesiastical settlements they sought to impose varied dramatically from reign to reign,

9

but in England and Wales they generally succeeded in enforcing a fair degree of conformity, on a temporary basis at least. In Ireland, by contrast, the royal administration failed to secure the religious submission of the bulk of the population.

Many of those who struggled on opposite sides of religious divides during these years shared the conviction that some form of religious uniformity should be enforced. Scottish Presbyterians and Episcopalians in the seventeenth century, for example, did not differ on the principle of one national Church for all, although they were radically opposed to one another over the form of government that Church should have. At the same time, however, there also emerged minority Christian groups who criticized the very basis of the social cohesion argument. One of the earliest protests against its coercive implications was made in 1612 by the Baptist writer Thomas Helwys. He based his case on the need to safeguard not only the freedom of the creature but also that of the Creator:

> For our Lord the King is but an earthly King, and if the Kings people be obedient and true subjects, obeying all humane laws made by the King, our Lord the King can require no more. For mens religion to God is betwixt God and themselves; the King shall not answer for it, neither may the King be judge betwene God and man. Let them be heretikes, Turks, Jewes, or whatsoever, it apperteynes not to the earthly power to punish them in the least measure.[2]

The social cohesion argument for religious uniformity has been irreversibly eroded in Western Europe through the growing recognition of religious diversity as a fundamental feature of society. This recognition, with its eventual corollaries of religious freedom and the removal of religious discrimination, was achieved in different ways in these islands. In England and Wales, there was a gradual removal of restrictions on the religious and civil rights first of Protestant Nonconformists, and later of Jews and Roman Catholics. In Scotland, the process of according full toleration to Episcopalians and Roman Catholics only began after the removal of the threat of Jacobitism, which they were perceived to support. The situation in Ireland was particularly bitterly contested, with a minority Protestant ascendancy only belatedly acknowledging the rights first of Presbyterians and then of the majority Roman Catholic population.

As the nature of society further diversified during the twentieth century, the safeguarding of religious freedom became positively established as a fundamental principle throughout our four nations, as generally in post-war Western Europe. This principle encompasses not only the historic world faiths but also New Religious Movements, though in some cases arguments of social welfare continue to be advanced against full recognition of some NRMs. The idea has also been extended, under the rubric of 'Freedom of Religion or Belief', to include protection of the rights of those who hold non-religious beliefs, or indeed beliefs antithetical to religion. In England and Scotland, this guarantee of free religious diversity has taken place in the context of continuing public acknowledgement of one or other form of the Christian Church (Anglican or Presbyterian, respectively) as having a special place in national life.

Alongside these socio-political arguments, Churches in the past have also been reluctant to accord freedom of expression to different beliefs on more strictly theological grounds. The premise for this second argument was that the conflict of the Church's understanding of the truth of the Christian faith with the tenets of deviant beliefs shows that the latter are false. In that case, it was argued, to encourage, or even to permit, the propagation of false beliefs would be to condone a public offence against the truth made known by God. The Church should therefore actively press the state, wherever possible, to suppress the manifestation of such error. As in the case of the social uniformity argument, this theological stance was generally first developed in disputes between Christians of different traditions. It was only later that it came to be extended to other religions and belief systems.

The best-known formulation of this position was undoubtedly the pre-Vatican II Roman Catholic insistence that 'error has no rights'. A demand for the elimination of religious error from public life was here premised on a firm conviction of the objective truth of the Catholic faith. Equally, that truth was seen to require the freedom of the Catholic Church to propagate its life and teachings in all situations. Accordingly, official Catholicism adopted a double approach to issues of religious toleration, according to the context in question. Thus, on the one hand, it maintained that a non-Catholic state was objectively obliged to safeguard freedom of religious life for Catholics. On the other hand, a Catholic state was under no such obligation with regard to non-Catholic communities. In 1864 Pope Pius IX emphasized the latter point in his 'Syllabus of Errors'. This document condemned 80 selected propositions, among which were the following 'errors of liberalism':

[77] In our age, it is no longer advisable that the Catholic religion be the only State religion (*unica status religio*), excluding all the other cults.

[78] Therefore it is praiseworthy that in some Catholic regions the law has allowed people immigrating there to exercise publicly their own cult.[3]

Contemporary Christian attitudes

The growth of ecumenism, developing attitudes to inter faith relations, and changes in society have all been factors contributing to the abandonment of this theological position. Positively, it could be said that the Churches have been led into a deeper understanding of the meaning of religious freedom. The change was perhaps most dramatically seen in the Roman Catholic Church. In 1965, the Second Vatican Council's 'Declaration on Religious Freedom', *Dignitatis Humanae*, asserted:

> The human person has a right to religious freedom. This freedom means that all men are to be immune from coercion on the part of individuals, social groups and every human power so that, within due limits, nobody is forced to act against his convictions in religious matters in private or in public, alone or in associations with others.[4]

This declaration radically reinterpreted Catholic teaching on civil rights in regard to religious diversity.[5] The previous double approach, distinguishing between Catholic and non-Catholic states, was now replaced by a universal insistence on the importance of religious freedom for all in every context. Nevertheless, it would be false to conclude that the Council's affirmation of religious liberty was based on a theological assumption that the beliefs of all religions are equally true, or their practices equally valid. Opposition to 'indifferentism' of this kind had certainly influenced Pius IX's 'Syllabus', but it is equally clearly to be found in modern Catholic teaching. Defence of the right to belong to a certain religion should not be confused with a positive judgement of the truth or value of that religion:

> The right to religious liberty is neither a moral licence to adhere to error, nor a supposed right to error, but rather a natural right of the human person to civil liberty.[6]

This points to a matter of fundamental importance for all Christians in their attitudes to people of differing beliefs, whether those be other Christians, members of other world religions, or people of no religious belief. To insist that all should have an equal right to hold and to express their own beliefs is not the same as to suggest that those beliefs are all on the same level of truth. Equally, to repudiate discrimination against people or communities on the grounds of their beliefs is not to pass any judgement on the validity of those beliefs. On the contrary, as an atmosphere of religious freedom will allow for the open expression of disagreement, we may expect it to lead to vigorous debate and exchange of views between those who believe differently. Indeed, for Christians committed to inter faith dialogue, this is precisely one reason why it is so important to combat any form of religious discrimination.

Religions not only involve beliefs; they also require or encourage particular patterns of behaviour. It is where faith flows into ethics and practice that concrete problems may arise over the boundaries of religious freedom. Clearly, Christians should not seek the prohibition of certain practices *just because* they are the consequences of particular beliefs. That would be to discriminate directly against the 'manifestation' of that religion.[7] However, there may be situations where attempts are made to justify, by an appeal to religious freedom, behaviour which would normally be unacceptable.

The need for some limits on the manifestation of religion or belief is recognized in Article 9 (2) of the European Convention on Human Rights:

> Freedom to manifest one's religion or beliefs shall be subject only to such limitations as are prescribed by law and are necessary in a democratic society in the interests of public safety, for the protection of public order, health or morals, or for the protection of the rights and freedoms of others.

The practical application of this general principle will ultimately be a question to be decided by the courts in the light of any relevant legal provisions, on a case-by-case basis. Few people will want to argue that religious freedom should in itself constitute a justification for behaviour that would otherwise be impermissible. Christians will have their own views on where behaviour crosses this boundary line. The law needs to reflect the view of society as a whole.

It is a matter for debate how far a broad moral consensus can be established in a plural society as a basis for guidance in these questions. Some would argue that key ethical values found in Christianity are shared across the world's faiths, as well as being accepted by many without any formal religious commitment. For example, no appeal to religious freedom should be allowed to justify practices that cause harm to others; that exploit or endanger children or other vulnerable members of society; or that remove people's freedom to change their religion. However, these are very wide-ranging issues that cannot be explored fully in this document. The point to be noted here is simply that an absolute right to freedom of religion or belief is not the same as an unqualified licence to act in pursuit of that religion or belief.

Theological foundations

In place of the discredited claim that 'error has no rights', the Churches today are seeking theological arguments by which to ground their commitment to the principle of religious freedom firmly in the core affirmations of Christian faith. A range of positions can be found here, but all stress in common the dignity of the human person. Men and women are created in the image of God, and entrusted by God with the freedom to quest for meaning and purpose in life, both individually and in community. From such a perspective, any curtailment of this freedom is potentially an encroachment on the prerogatives of the God who gives freedom – as Thomas Helwys pointed out four hundred years ago.

Dignitatis Humanae itself develops this kind of approach in a way that gives particular emphasis to the role of religious identity in human self-understanding. The declaration argues that, as men and women are created in the image of God and designed for communion with God, the religious dimension of their existence is an inviolable aspect of their human dignity. Indeed, it is that by which they seek to orient themselves to God, and therefore has a transcendent goal. It follows that religious identity must have an importance greater than that of other aspects of human life. This in turn means that it is deserving of special public acknowledgement and protection:

> The private and public acts of religion by which men direct themselves to God according to their convictions transcend of their very nature the earthly and temporal order of things. Government therefore ought indeed to take account of the religious life of the citizenry and show it favour.[8]

For Christians, it is the life, death and resurrection of Jesus of Nazareth that provide the supreme norm for faith and behaviour. His ministry demonstrates a respect for the inviolability of the individual's inner judgement guided by conscience, and acknowledges the impossibility of coercing authentic belief. His call to discipleship, while categorical for those who are chosen, finds expression in terms of attraction and invitation:

> Come to me, all you that are weary and are carrying heavy burdens, and I will give you rest. Take my yoke upon you and learn from me; for I am gentle and humble in heart, and you will find rest for your souls. For my yoke is easy and my burden is light.[9]

Jesus' witness to the truth of God also recognizes the reality of secular authority, but insists that any political power must ultimately be subject to the inner summons addressed by God to the human person. This is an insistence most powerfully enacted in the drama of his trial and crucifixion:

My kingdom is not from this world. If my kingdom were from this world, my followers would be fighting ... You say that I am a king. For this I was born, and for this I came into the world, to testify to the truth. Everyone who belongs to the truth listens to my voice.[10]

In turn, the apostolic proclamation of the crucified and risen Christ, while emphasizing the urgency of the opportunity offered by God, is always presented as good news, which people may choose to accept or to reject.[11] From the beginnings of Christian faith, then, a recognition of the integrity of the other's religious identity can be said to have been implicit in the Church's mission. From this perspective, the emphasis on religious freedom in contemporary Christianity is not so much an innovation as a recovering of a forgotten truth.

Nevertheless, on a Christian view, although religious identity is inviolable, it is not immutable. The basis of religious freedom lies in human beings' creation by a God who invites them into communion with himself. As individuals travel on their journey with and to this God, their inward convictions will almost certainly change and develop. Religious identity, therefore, must be understood in ways that take account of this development and change.

For some people at some times, the extent of change may be such that they come to a decision to make a socially visible transfer from identification with one faith community to membership of another. Thus freedom of religion in Christian understanding includes freedom to change religion. This can, of course, be a very sensitive issue, as conversion has implications not only for individuals but for whole families and communities.[12] However, the missionary character of the Christian faith means that religious identity cannot be adequately understood as an inherited and static categorization. Christians today would insist that the right of all to change their religion or belief is an essential component of full religious freedom.

Religious freedom in Christian understanding and in human rights

In insisting that freedom to change religion is an essential component of freedom of religion, a Christian understanding is in line with the general development of contemporary thinking about human rights. In particular, it coheres with the European Convention on Human Rights that, through the Human Rights Act 1998, has since autumn 2000 been incorporated into UK law. Article 9 (1) of the Declaration, on 'Freedom of Thought, Conscience and Religion', reads as follows:

> Everyone has the right to freedom of thought, conscience and religion; this right includes freedom to change his religion or belief and freedom, either alone or in community with others and in public or private, to manifest his religion or belief, in worship, teaching, practice and observance.

The Churches will support this assertion of the right to freedom of religion and belief, then, for reasons deeply rooted in a Christian understanding of the dignity and vocation of the human person, as individual and in community. However, there are two respects in which a Christian position would want to amplify this statement.

In the first place, the 'manifestation' of Christian religion cannot for Christians be divorced from the mission of God in the world, in whatever terms this may be expressed. Although the understanding and practice of mission vary immensely between and within contemporary Christian Churches, there is a consensus that 'freedom to manifest' religion implies 'freedom to propagate' religion. Of course, such a freedom would extend not only to Christian mission but also to the activities of other communities in propagating their religions or beliefs.

In some cases, 'propagation' of a religion is primarily directed towards bringing about the conversion of people from one religious group to another. This can lead people in one community to feel that the 'protection of their rights and freedoms' requires some curtailment of the propagation of beliefs by the other community. Tensions of this sort can and do occur between different Christian traditions as well as between different faiths. However, there is a clear danger here that legitimate witness and evangelism may be inhibited, particularly if considerations of 'public order or morals' are advanced by the state as justifying limitations on this way of manifesting a religion.[13] It has in any case been argued that legal interpretation of the ECHR provisions has generally been unduly deferential to the interests of the state.[14] The Churches' emphasis on the centrality of mission could provide an important check to such tendencies.

A second distinctive Christian contribution to the understanding of religious freedom is to recognize the importance of communities as well as individuals. The biblical account stresses that human persons are created in and for relationship and communion, both temporally and eternally. Religious identity is not limited to a private choice, but rather leads naturally to participation in public religious communities as the authentic expression of the inward impulse of faith. This implies a responsibility on governments to safeguard the religious freedom of organized communities as well as of individuals. Without such communal protection, the individual's right to religious freedom cannot be realistically exercised.

In practical terms, there will be occasions where protecting the freedom of a religious community will involve allowing that community to impose within the ordering of its own life some restrictive conditions based on religion. To give an obvious and uncontested example, a church, mosque or synagogue must be able to require of any individual to be appointed as a minister, imam or rabbi that they should (at the least) be a Christian, Muslim or Jew respectively. Situations of this kind raise complex issues that we discuss further below, both as they affect the Churches (Chapter 3) and as they must be dealt with in the framing of legislation (Chapter 4).

Religious freedom in a multi-faith world

We have argued that the Churches can establish a strong position, rooted in core affirmations of Christian faith and reflecting an ecumenical consensus, in defence of religious freedom, and so against religious discrimination. The case builds on a theological understanding of religious freedom as a basic right that arises from the created dignity and divine vocation of human persons. It encompasses the freedom to hold, to manifest, to propagate, and to change religion. Through the wider idea of belief, its scope embraces freedom from religion as well as freedom of religion. It is applicable at different levels to both individuals and communities. It incorporates and builds upon the principles set out in the European Convention on Human Rights.

Much of this position would be held in common with people of other faiths, though of course they would support their case with different religious arguments. On some points, though, there is no consensus between the religions. In some traditions, freedom to propagate religion is opposed as giving licence to attack traditionally established faiths and pressure people into conversion. In others, freedom to change religion is not accepted as it is seen as giving permission to apostasy.[15] Christians in some parts of the world are caught up in conflicts over issues such as these. In these islands, where Christians can play a formative role in helping to shape the framework of a religiously plural society, the Churches can perhaps help these difficult situations by demonstrating their clear commitment to a principled defence of religious freedom and fairness for all.

17

Chapter Three

The Churches and religious discrimination

The principle of religious freedom, for which we have argued on theological grounds in the previous chapter, needs to be applied by the Churches to the question of religious discrimination in our own societies. In this chapter, we first highlight the contemporary factors that make this a matter of particular urgency today. We then outline some of the practical ways in which the Churches can respond.

Religious discrimination in Britain and Ireland today

The Churches share, with others, in the goal of building inclusive societies in which people of all backgrounds can participate fully as citizens. For this to happen, Christians today recognize that they need to repudiate the racial prejudice and discrimination that have disfigured both Church and society. The work of the Churches' Commission for Racial Justice (CCRJ) is one important example of the lead that Christians are now giving in the fight against racism.[1] For many individuals and communities, though, racial and religious dimensions of their identity are inextricably intertwined. This can have the negative consequence that people experience a double sense of discrimination. The Derby Project found, for instance, that a majority of respondents from black-led Churches reported that 'ethnic or racial grounds' were a large part of the reason for the unfair treatment that they experienced on the basis of religion.[2] There is a sense, then, in which the Churches' commitment to racial justice will inevitably lead them to address issues of religious discrimination also.

During the last decade of the twentieth century, issues of specifically religious identity surfaced in two highly contentious disputes in Britain: the protests among Muslims over Salman Rushdie's book *The Satanic Verses* (published in 1988), and the pressure from Hindus for planning permission to use Bhaktivedanta Manor near Watford as a place of worship (eventually granted in 1995). A long, and ultimately successful, campaign by the faith communities also led to questions on religious affiliation being included in the 2001 Census both in England and Wales and in Scotland. Yet the discourse of community relations is only just coming to terms with these and similar developments marking the reappearance of religious categories of identity as major factors in public debate:

> In the latter half of this [20th] century, public policy throughout Britain has largely engaged with issues arising from religious plurality in a way characterised by responses to 'racial' and ethnic diversity. Consideration of the implications of the extended plurality of contemporary British society has not always clearly identified or taken account of the issues arising from specifically religious, rather than broadly ethnic and cultural, plurality.[3]

The *Satanic Verses* and Bhaktivedanta Manor cases highlighted issues of religion in relation to public authorities, and this is one area where religious discrimination may occur. As the largest faith communities in these islands, and with a long history of interaction with society at all levels, the Christian Churches are well placed to interpret in a wider context the importance of protecting in a public context the religious identity of individuals and communities. However, it is also important to recognize that discrimination can arise between different religions. Here again, the Churches can make a major positive contribution by drawing on the lessons gained from their own, often painful, experiences of religious discrimination between different Christian traditions.

The Churches' commitment to justice provides a further motivation for taking the question of religious discrimination seriously. Existing legal provisions in Great Britain demonstrate *prima facie* inconsistencies in the treatment of different groups. Case law has established, for instance, that the religious rights of Sikhs and Jews are afforded some protection under the Race Relations Act. This is because their faith allegiance coincides with their ethnic identity, meaning that they can be classed in legal terms as 'religio-ethnic groups' that satisfy the two essential criteria for coverage by the Act:

> A long shared history, of which the group is conscious as distinguishing it from other groups, and the memory of which it keeps alive;

and

> a cultural tradition of its own, including family and social customs and manners, often but not necessarily associated with religious observance.[4]

However, several cases have also shown that no such direct protection exists in English law for Muslims on the basis of their religious identity. This is because Islam, like Christianity or Buddhism, is the faith of a multi-ethnic community. Consequently, the only redress open to Muslims who feel that they are victims of religious discrimination is by a claim of indirect racial discrimination. Even this, though, is an option only open to those from an ethnic or national origin which is predominantly Muslim, and cases of this kind have proved difficult to establish.

The Churches' commitment to positive inter faith relations also challenges Christians to take to heart the strength of feeling around issues of religious discrimination in many communities. For example, the then Secretary General of the Muslim Council of Britain said, in a speech before the Prime Minister in 1999:

> Religious discrimination is real. It happens. And worse is vilification of religious sanctities. And it hurts. A law against religious discrimination and religious vilification may not eliminate the problem. But it would be a clear statement of policy of what is not acceptable in a civilised society.[5]

The complex issues raised by legislation are discussed in the next chapter, but there is evident in these words a deeper appeal, shared by others as well as Muslims: to take seriously the implications of their understanding of themselves as people and as communities of faith. This is surely an appeal to which Christians can respond positively through their own commitment to combat religious discrimination. As such discrimination generally appears within a range of other hostile or unfair ways of treating people on the grounds of their religion, the Churches' response must be on several different levels. In particular, we now move on to consider how:

- to dispel religious prejudice, Churches can educate their members and the wider public about different faiths;

- to break down hatred or suspicion against people of other religions, Churches can share in the task of establishing positive inter faith relations;

- to address religious disadvantage, Churches can act as advocates for access by all faith communities to a place in public life; and

- to demonstrate ways of tackling discrimination within organizations, Churches can review their own arrangements so as to become exemplars of good practice.

Educating people about different faiths

Christians are bidden not to 'bear false witness' against their neighbours. In a religiously plural society, this translates into a positive injunction to be accurate and truthful about the beliefs and practices of people of different faiths. The Churches' responsibility here is to combat misinformation, prejudice and bigotry, whether such attitudes are expressed by church members or within wider society. In this educational task, the Churches can exercise considerable influence through their substantial presence in primary and secondary schools (for example in the content and delivery of RE and citizenship curricula), through their contacts with media at local and national levels, and through the respect and trust that church leaders generally enjoy within the community.

A particularly important challenge of this kind was highlighted by the Runnymede Trust's 1997 report on 'Islamophobia' that drew attention to widespread evidence of stereotyping and hostility towards Muslims in key areas of British society. Among the 'recommendations to non-Muslim faith communities' were the following:

- Leaders to accept that they have a major responsibility for reducing Islamophobia, and for in no way giving encouragement to it.

- Routinely complain to the Press Complaints Commission and to the newspapers concerned when they consider that coverage of Islam or of Muslims has been inaccurate, misleading or distorted.

- Discuss Islamophobia directly, and to incorporate reference to Islamophobia into their guidelines and policy documents.[6]

The report was quite clear that not all criticism of Islam or of Muslims was to be labelled as 'Islamophobic'. The root of the problem, it suggested, was to be found in depicting Islam as a single undifferentiated system, so failing to recognize the great variety of views to be found among Muslims.

The subsequent Runnymede Trust report, *The Future of Multi-Ethnic Britain*, pointed out that the distinction of 'closed' and 'open' views could similarly be applied to attitudes towards any example of 'the Other'. 'Closed' views caricatured the Other as 'a single monolithic bloc, static and unresponsive to new realities'. By contrast, 'open' views recognized the Other as 'diverse and progressive, with internal differences, debates and development'.[7] Part of the Churches' vocation is surely to develop religious literacy in society through giving people awareness of diversity through open views of other religions and beliefs. Equally, the Churches can reasonably expect people in other communities not to caricature or stereotype Christian beliefs and attitudes.

In some situations, the Churches themselves bear a historical responsibility for fostering negative and inaccurate images of other faith communities, and so are challenged all the more strongly to address the misleading and hostile stereotypes that survive within their own life. The most obvious example of this is doubtless the painful history of Jewish–Christian relations. Through the ages an ecclesiastically sanctioned 'teaching of contempt' has contributed to the growth of popular antisemitism in European society, with disastrous consequences. There is a continuing need to reshape Christian attitudes and practices to overcome this legacy and to recognize the continuing vitality of Judaism today.[8] In this and similar contexts where whole groups of people have been calumniated or abused in the name of Christian teaching and values, Pope John Paul II has spoken of the need for a 'purification of memory':

> an act of courage and humility in recognising the wrongs done by those who have borne or bear the name of Christian.[9]

Building inter faith relations

Participating in the development of positive inter faith relations at every level is critically important in addressing religious discrimination. Religious differences can easily become causes of the division and suspicion that feed religious hatred. This can best be overcome by the creation of safe spaces where people of different faiths are able to share their experiences and insights together and so to build up a sense of shared trust and mutual respect. The aim of such sharing is not the elimination of differences. Nor can it rest content simply with the identification of common ground between different faiths – indeed, one test of maturity in any inter faith relationship is the ability to deal with sincere and radical disagreement. Dialogue of this kind can be a painful and lengthy process, but it brings immense benefits both for immediate participants and for the wider community:

> Living and working together is not always easy. Religion harnesses deep emotions which can sometimes take destructive forms. Where this happens, we must draw on our faith to bring about reconciliation and understanding. The truest fruits of religion are healing and positive. We have a great deal to learn from one another which can enrich us without undermining our identities. Together, listening with openness and respect, we can move forward to work in ways that acknowledge genuine differences but build on shared hopes and values.[10]

Christian participation in inter faith dialogue springs from convictions rooted in the very heart of the gospel: love of neighbour, sharing in reconciliation, witness to truth, openness to the Spirit.[11] However, these attitudes cannot be simply assumed among Christians. Inter faith work requires substantial resources of time, energy, finance and prayer to bear fruit. By contrast, where there is no commitment to dialogue, there will always be a danger of religious separatism and mutual enmity developing. A multi-faith society is not guaranteed inter faith harmony without substantial and costly effort.

Advocacy and access

Churches can also act in partnership with others as advocates of a recognized place for the spiritual in public life. Through its long history in these islands, Christianity has access to civil governance and institutions at many different levels. This is most visibly evident constitutionally, in the established position of the Church of England and the special status of the Church of Scotland within their respective nations. Beyond this, though, all the historic Churches as a whole can be broadly said to share in an 'informal establishment' which is expressed in such features as: access to and influence on decision-making individuals and organizations in public life, publicly funded institutional chaplaincies, or the marking of major national and local events by civic acts of worship. From the Churches' point of view, such arrangements are not seen as signs of power or prestige. Rather, they are welcomed as opportunities to demonstrate Christian concern for, and service of, all parts of society.

However, this may not match the understanding of religious groups not fully included in these networks, whether these be other faiths or newer Churches. From their perspective, there may be a sense of exclusion or disadvantage that can contribute to an awareness of religious discrimination. In recent years, feelings like this have been expressed from different quarters in relation to such diverse issues as: chaplaincy arrangements for non-Christian prisoners; representation of faith communities in the House of Lords; state funding of religious schools; or visible participation of minority groups in Remembrance Day ceremonies.

On the other hand, a process of wider pluralization and inclusiveness in public life has also been evident in a number of areas. These include: the growth of multi-faith chaplaincy teams in many hospitals; the planning of local agreed syllabuses for RE by conferences drawing on representatives of all faith communities; or the arrangements for the Millennium Dome 'Faith Zone' brokered by the Lambeth Group of Churches and other faiths. Successful outcomes such as these have been achieved by the Churches not withdrawing from public involvement, but rather opening up to other faith communities sources of access and expertise, acting as their advocates where they have been excluded, and forging strong bonds of working partnership with them on practical projects. Adjusting to ever-changing situations of this kind will continue to be a challenge for the Churches, especially those that historically have had the greatest investment in public life. The Christian vocation to serve the common good would be distorted if it were to be exercised in an exclusive or patronizing way. It would be entirely perverted if it were to become an inadvertent factor in perpetuating religious disadvantage or exclusion.

Good practice

The Churches' concern to combat religious discrimination will also have implications for their own life, and for the life of the organizations for which they are responsible. Identifying good practice in this area is a more complex issue than, for example, in the case of racial discrimination. As the Christian community is called to be a multi-ethnic fellowship and sign of the unity of all God's people, a commitment to racial justice clearly rules out any justification whatsoever for discrimination on the part of the Church. In the multi-religious situation, though, the corporate freedom of the Church to maintain its own Christian identity needs to be protected, and this will inevitably lead to some situations where Churches and other Christian organizations will wish to impose restrictions based on religion in various areas of their life. Such restrictions can technically be described as themselves instances of religious discrimination. However, it is important to recognize that they are only in place to ensure freedom from discrimination for the organization as a whole. On a Christian view, religious freedom needs protecting for communities as well as for individuals. These two interests can in some situations come into conflict, especially over patterns of behaviour that may be considered as either required or excluded by the maintenance of a Christian ethos. Parallel concerns of this kind are of course to be found in other faith communities as well.

Among Christians, there is in practice a considerable variety of approaches to these issues. In the important area of employment policy, all would agree that certain posts require evident participation in the life of a Christian community as a 'genuine occupational qualification'.[12] The case of ordained ministers of the various Churches is an obvious example; indeed, a specific denominational allegiance is usually also necessary here. Teachers responsible for Christian religious instruction in Church schools would be another generally accepted example. Some Christian organizations would then extend a restrictive approach of this kind to all their posts by operating a policy of employing exclusively Christians. Their justification would be that this was essential to preserve the character, motivation and coherence of the organization. Other Christian organizations, by contrast, would be happy to employ non-Christians in a wide range of roles. Their argument might be that the resultant diversity of their staff was itself a sign of Christian belief in the God-given dignity of all.

Religiously based restrictions may also be an issue in the provision of goods and services. Here again the questions facing the Churches are complex. For example, debates have arisen over the letting of church halls for the use of other religious groups, over the disposal of redundant church buildings to other religious communities, and over the involvement of representatives of other religions in the management of church-related community organizations. Issues such as these have all been resolved in different ways by different Churches. At the local level there may indeed be further considerable variation even within one Christian denomination.[13]

Important issues of this kind also arise in relation to schools with a religious foundation, an increasing number of which are supported by public funding. Again, a range of views can be found in the Churches, though all emphasize that schools of any kind should meet agreed standards of curriculum and ethos. Some Christians are uncomfortable with the idea of state support for any schools affiliated to particular faiths, as they see this as potentially fostering division within society. Given governmental funding for schools of some religious traditions, though, they might add that there is a strong natural justice argument for saying that provision should be made equitably across religious distinctions. Others see Church schools as a vitally important part of the Churches' mission in the world, through the role they can play in spreading Christian values more widely. Others again see the role of the Christian school in terms of nurturing the young people of a given Christian tradition, and so helping to protect its continuing identity. At times in our history, disputes over the public support of different forms of Christian education have been bitter, contributing significantly to intra-Christian sectarianism.

In the new situation of religious pluralism also, questions relating to Church schools continue to raise dilemmas for the Churches. One issue, for example, concerns the admissions policies of Church schools in areas with very high proportions of children from non-Christian faith backgrounds. Should these favour, exclusively or predominantly, students from Christian homes, with the aim of providing an unambiguously Christian educational environment? Or, alternatively, should admissions reflect the ethnic and cultural profile of the local community – bearing in mind that this may result in Christian foundations with very high proportions of pupils from other faith backgrounds? Both these approaches can be found, as can attempts to strike some kind of a balance between the two. Local churches in such situations may also feel that they have a particular responsibility towards the educational needs of Christian families, of whatever race, who live effectively as minorities in neighbourhoods predominantly of other faiths. These are issues which are likely to become of still greater significance in the UK given the Government's renewed emphasis on the part that Church schools can play in overall educational provision.

Within all this diversity of Christian thought and practice, it is nevertheless possible to identify some generally applicable points of good practice. The following are five principles on which we believe Christians of all viewpoints should be able to agree:

- If a Christian organization excludes or restricts non-Christians in certain situations, the reasons for this should be clearly stated in relation to the organization's overall understanding of its character and mission, and clearly and courteously communicated to those affected.

- Particularly cogent explanations will need to be made when an organization is in receipt of public funding, or where it relies heavily on the goodwill of non-Christian supporters. It is likely that the providers of such support will want to be reassured that the organization's work is not exclusive or sectarian in its approach.

- The appearance and reality of internal discrimination within organizations need to be avoided. If some senior positions are reserved for Christians but an equal opportunities policy operates for other posts, it may be necessary to give careful thought to staff development structures if there is not to be a sense of unfairness and frustration. Parallel tensions can arise when some of an organization's services are open to all, and others are restricted to Christians.

- Where people of other faiths participate in Christian organizations, whether as employees, pupils, clients, service users, or in any other way, care must be taken to ensure that their religious and spiritual needs are recognized and appropriately met.

- It is important to ensure, so far as this is possible, that any Christian organization's policies and practices do not result in people of other faiths being treated in a way that seems unfair when compared to the treatment of other non-Christians of no particular religious allegiance. Failures in this respect can be deeply hurtful to people of other faiths, and understandably add to their sense of discrimination, particularly if they perceive that there may also be an overlap with discrimination on racial grounds.

CHAPTER FOUR

The law and religious discrimination

In this chapter, we turn to the issues raised for the Churches by legislation on religious discrimination. This is not the only legal question in relation to religious identity. For example, there is in Great Britain no general prohibition of incitement to religious hatred. The common law offence of blasphemy in English law refers to abusive attacks on the Christian religion only, and more particularly on the beliefs of the established Church of England.[1] The failure of an attempt by Muslims to bring a prosecution for blasphemy against the publishers of Salman Rushdie's *The Satanic Verses*[2] demonstrated the lack of protection this law affords for non-Christians, and it has been suggested that this is demonstrably unfair.[3] While some have argued for abolition of the offence of blasphemy without replacement, others have called for new legislation that would protect people of all faiths.[4] Others again have counselled that, despite its inequality, the present law at least provides some measure of protection for religious identity in public life. There seems to be no consensus on this question, either among the Churches or within wider society.

Religious discrimination: the legal situation

Currently, legislation against discrimination on the grounds of religion or belief is in place in these islands only in the Republic of Ireland[5] and in Northern Ireland.[6] In England, Wales and Scotland, there is no generally applicable and direct legal protection from religious discrimination.[7] However, two recent developments are highlighting the need for a fresh approach in this area: the incorporation into British law of the European Convention on Human Rights (operative throughout the UK since October 2000 through the Human Rights Act 1998), and the obligation on all EU countries to implement by December 2003 a community directive on equal treatment in employment.[8]

The Human Rights Act provides for the enforcement in UK courts of the rights guaranteed by the European Convention on Human Rights, and makes it unlawful for public authorities to act in a way incompatible with those rights. This is a significant step forward in the protection of religious freedom, as Article 9 of the ECHR is a clear assertion of 'freedom of thought, conscience and religion'.[9] Some further measure of protection specifically from religious discrimination is provided by Article 14:

> The enjoyment of the rights and freedoms set forth in this Convention shall be secured without discrimination on any ground such as sex, race ... religion ... or other status.

However, as its wording shows, Article 14 is ancillary to the other ECHR rights; it does not in itself provide a free-standing protection against religious discrimination.[10] Since, moreover, the Human Rights Act applies only to public authorities, its overall effect in combating religious discrimination seems to be limited.

Under the Treaty of Amsterdam, the European Union in November 2000 adopted a directive requiring member countries to provide for equal treatment in employment and occupation 'without discrimination on grounds of religion or belief, disability, age, or sexual orientation'.[11] The directive also includes complex provisions allowing for exemptions in the case of Churches and other religious bodies, to ensure that they would be in a position legally to impose restrictions on grounds of religion or belief in the case of certain appointments.[12]

The European Employment Directive provides a clear motivation for the introduction of legislation prohibiting religious discrimination, but important questions about its implementation remain open at this stage.[13] Some concern the scope of any legislation: should it be restricted to employment; or should it cover wider areas (as does current Race Relations law)? Others concern its relation to other pieces of anti-discrimination legislation: should there be a specific Religious Discrimination Act; an amendment to the Race Relations Act; or a single Equality Act covering all grounds of unlawful discrimination? Corresponding to these legislative options, how should legislation be enforced: by a newly formed 'Commission for Religious Relations'; by an extended Commission for Racial Equality; or by a unified Equality (or Human Rights) Commission? On these and other practical issues, it will be important for the Churches – together with other faith communities – to be involved in close and detailed consultation over the shaping of the new legislation. Christians would approach this with a fundamentally positive attitude. Legislation against religious discrimination would not only remedy inconsistencies in current provisions, it would also affirm the importance of religious identity, and be a sign of a more inclusive society.

We can identify three particular areas where theological perspectives could help to shape Christian views on practical issues in the framing of legislation. First, there is the challenge of giving meaning to the term 'religion' in law. Second, there is the question of exemptions to allow religious organizations themselves legally to impose restrictions on the grounds of religion. Third, it is important that legislation designed to protect and affirm religious identity does not unintentionally contribute to division and distrust in society.

The meaning of religion

The difficulty of defining the term 'religion' has sometimes been advanced as a problem in framing any law on religious discrimination. In fact, because the 'advancement of religion' is recognized as a charitable purpose, some English case law has already been formulated on the meaning of 'religion', though considerable ambiguities and uncertainties remain.[14] Moreover, legislation against religious discrimination already exists in the Republic of Ireland, Northern Ireland and elsewhere[15] without encountering major problems through the difficulty of definition. Three distinct legislative approaches offer themselves as ways of tackling this problem: first, to include a definition of 'religion' within the initial framing of legislation; or second, to draw up an official list of recognized religions; or third, to leave the more precise delineation of the scope of religion to the work of the courts.

We have argued that a Christian approach to these issues will emphasize the centrality of religious freedom. It will recognize the fluid and dynamic nature of religious identity. It will distinguish sharply between defending the liberty of religious disagreement and asserting the triviality of religious difference: the right to hold any belief should not depend on the extent to which that belief resembles Christian (or any other) faith. This points to a rejection of any official 'listing' of religions, as that would run the risk both of fossilizing religious identity and of prejudging beliefs as more or less worthy of protection in the measure that they are more or less familiar. It also highlights the dangers of trying to provide any definition of religion that is not related to a case-by-case consideration of the actual beliefs and practices to which people subscribe in their religious lives.

The logic of our approach therefore favours the third route, of allowing the courts to develop a body of law defining the boundaries of religion where that proves necessary. It also suggests that legislation should be framed in such a way as to include not only religious faiths but also the wider sense of 'religious belief' that covers sincerely held positions opposed to religion such as atheism, humanism and agnosticism.[16] It does not logically follow, though, that protection would then be afforded by the same measure to all forms of 'belief' however widely defined – for example, including sincerely held political and ideological views.

Exemptions

An important issue in the framing of any legislation on religious discrimination involves exemptions for religious organizations, or organizations with particular links to religions. Such exemptions would give them the freedom legally to preserve their particular religious character through imposing religiously based restrictions in certain situations. The definition of such situations proved a contentious matter in the drafting of the European directive. The Irish Churches were among those particularly concerned that legislation should respect an organization's ethos based on religion or belief.[17] As a result of the scrutiny process, the draft directive was significantly amended to produce a complex text giving member states permission to recognize a much wider range of exemptions than originally allowed.[18]

Several interrelated questions will need to be addressed in translating this text into legislation. For example, what criteria should be used to determine which posts within an organization require subscription to a religion or belief as a 'genuine occupational qualification' for employment? If legislation were to cover the provision of goods and services, what exemptions would it be appropriate to allow in, say, the use or disposal of religious premises, or membership of religious clubs? To what extent should religious bodies be allowed to impose conditions on other grounds (such as gender or sexual orientation) where this is claimed to be necessary for them on religious or moral grounds?

Christians hold a wide range of views on these specific issues, but it should be possible to identify a shared starting-point in the underlying principles from which these questions are approached. Exemptions for churches and other religious organizations, although they will necessarily be framed in legal terms as permissions to practise religious discrimination, are ultimately designed to safeguard the religious freedom of communities as well as individuals. In approaching specific instances of possible exemption, therefore, the appropriate question for Christians to ask is this: 'Is it necessary to impose religiously based conditions in this situation in order to protect the Christian identity of this organization?' The range of answers which would emerge can then be understood as related to the range of views among Christians about the appropriate balance between corporate unity and individual diversity.[19]

The effects of legislation

There is a perceived danger that legislation might prove counter-productive, if it unintentionally contributed to division or distrust within society, rather than succeeding in its aim of respecting and protecting religious identity. Some have expressed the fear that the courts might find themselves being used to promote inter-religious and intra-religious rivalries. Others are concerned that measures to protect people of a particular faith from discrimination might be misunderstood as special treatment, and so end up generating hostility against that community. It has also been suggested that people might abuse the law by seeking to invent spurious religious obligations or identities for their own advantage. Such abuse could in turn discredit authentic religions.

One Christian response to such anxieties would be to emphasize the contextual and relational nature of religious discrimination. It involves the exclusion of people from full participation in a community (whether society, workplace, school, or whatever) on the grounds of their religious beliefs or practices. As such, it should be seen not so much as a falling short from an abstract standard of correct behaviour but rather as a failure to welcome in a generous and inclusive way people with those beliefs and practices. Conversely, a Christian attitude would welcome legislation that built on the concept of 'reasonable accommodation'.[20] That is to say, rather than a decontextualized norm of religious equality being imposed, a legal duty could be established for employers, public authorities and others to adjust their structures, practices and attitudes to meet the needs of the individuals and communities of different religious faiths and beliefs.

A Christian perspective would also frankly recognize the limitations of any legislation in modifying destructive behaviour. It is an insight deeply rooted in Christian faith that a law good in itself can perversely be distorted into an instrument of sin if divorced from its spiritual context. In practical terms, this points to the need to see legislation as only one element in an integrated approach to challenging religious discrimination. While a law can function both as an ultimate sanction and as an important declaratory statement of society's values, to transform people's attitudes and behaviour it needs to be complemented by education in inter-religious understanding, by the establishment of good inter-religious relations, and by the promotion of good practice in countering religious discrimination and safeguarding religious freedom. In all these areas, there is a crucially important role for Christians individually and for the Churches collectively to play in cooperation with other faith communities.

Finding some answers

Finally, we can return to the questions we posed at the outset, and suggest some ways of responding to them in the light of our arguments.

1 Why is religious discrimination a serious problem?

For many people in Britain and Ireland today, religion is one of the most important aspects of their identity. To build truly inclusive societies means enabling people of all religious faiths and beliefs to share fully as citizens in social, economic and cultural life. There is now evidence to show that significant groups of people feel that they cannot yet do this because of the unfair treatment that they experience on the grounds of their religion or belief. Tackling such discrimination is important for the health and harmony of all our communities.

2 Why should Christians be concerned about religious discrimination?

Christians today are committed to the principle of religious freedom. The God who made human beings in his own image desires that they may freely come to know and to rejoice in the truth. Christians need to treat others with respect for this God-given right, as Jesus showed in his relationships with people in the Gospels. Religious discrimination is a failure to take seriously one of the most important dimensions of our neighbours' lives.

3 Should not people of other faiths fit in when they come to live in Christian countries like ours?

Over the years, Christians of various traditions have learnt – sometimes painfully – to live with difference and diversity. In our own time, communities of other world faiths, many of whom have been living here for several generations, also contribute to the richness of our shared life. For people to participate fully in society, it is important that no aspect of their identity is excluded.

4   How can Christians treat people of other faiths equally if we believe that our religion is better than theirs?

Anyone committed to a religious faith will believe that faith to be true, and so will find it difficult to accept another faith as of equal value. However, there is a difference between considering other religions or beliefs to be of equal value and defending people's right to follow those religions or hold those beliefs. While many different views are to be found among Christians about the various faiths and beliefs encountered in our islands today, we need to honour and to protect the human dignity of all our fellow citizens equally, whatever their faith or belief.

5   Why should we protect the rights of minority faiths here when Christians are suffering overseas?

People of many different faiths suffer on account of their beliefs in various parts of the world. If Christians are to live up to the calling of Christ, they must be concerned about all these situations, and work for reconciliation and justice. A principled commitment to fighting religious discrimination here is one way in which British and Irish Christians may be able to help those in difficult situations in other countries.

6   Does not the law already provide protection against religious discrimination?

At present, legislation prohibiting discrimination on the grounds of religion or belief is in place in the Republic of Ireland. It is also in place in Northern Ireland, but in the rest of the United Kingdom there is no law to prevent religious discrimination (though the Race Relations Act does provide some limited protection to communities whose religious identity overlaps with a particular ethnic background). However, a European Union directive establishing an equal framework for opportunities in employment has to be implemented in EU member states by late 2003. Among other things, this will require legislation against religious discrimination in the area of employment or occupation.

7   Might not a law against religious discrimination cause more problems than it solves?

Religious identity is a complex and sensitive area, and it is important that new legislation should be carefully drafted, in close consultation with the Churches and other faith communities. Laws prohibiting religious discrimination on both sides of the border in Ireland have relied on a case-by-case approach to addressing problems, and this has generally proved successful. In Great Britain, the absence to date of any law on religious discrimination has caused problems for several communities. Legislation by itself will in any case be ineffective unless it is backed up by education, the encouragement of good practice, and the continuing development of positive inter faith relations.

8 Would a law against religious discrimination mean that Christian organizations could no longer insist on appointing only Christians to such posts as ministers or teachers?

Organizations of several different kinds aim to maintain an ethos based on a particular religion or belief. Any law will have to provide exemptions for such organizations, so that they can insist that certain posts can only be filled by people holding that religion or belief. The Churches, with other faith communities, have already made this point forcefully, and scope for exemptions is allowed in the European Employment Directive, as well as in existing laws in both Irish jurisdictions.

9 Would a law against religious discrimination mean that people could not criticize one another's beliefs?

Protecting people from discrimination on the grounds of their religion or belief does not imply protecting that religion or belief from public criticism. On the contrary, religious freedom allows for the open expression of disagreement and vigorous debate between people of different faiths and of none. At the same time, it is important that such an exchange of views be conducted in a peaceful and respectful spirit. A law on religious discrimination would not in itself cover the area of incitement to religious hatred, where legislation would raise further complex questions (for example, in relation to English law on blasphemy).

10 Would a law against religious discrimination unfairly favour people of other faiths?

Legislation would need to provide equal protection to people of all religions and beliefs. This would mean that Christians as well as people of other faiths could find legal redress if they experienced discrimination on the basis of their religion. As a law would identify the prohibited grounds of discrimination as 'religion or belief', it would also cover the rights of atheists, agnostics, humanists, and others holding beliefs opposed to religious faith.

Extracts from legal texts referred to in the report

1
European Convention on Human Rights (1950)

Article 9

(1) Everyone has the right to freedom of thought, conscience and religion; this right includes freedom to change his religion or belief and freedom, either alone or in community with others and in public or private, to manifest his religion or belief, in worship, teaching, practice and observance.

(2) Freedom to manifest one's religion or beliefs shall be subject only to such limitations as are prescribed by law and are necessary in a democratic society in the interests of public safety, for the protection of public order, health or morals, or for the protection of the rights and freedoms of others.

Article 14

The enjoyment of the rights and freedoms set forth in this Convention shall be secured without discrimination on any ground such as sex, race, colour, language, religion, political or other opinion, national or social origin, association with a national minority, property, birth, or other status.

2
[UK] Human Rights Act (1998)

Section 13: (1)

(1) If a court's determination of any question arising under this Act might affect the exercise by a religious organisation (itself or its members

collectively) of the Convention right to freedom of thought, conscience and religion, it must have particular regard to the importance of that right.

3
Northern Ireland Act (1998)

Section 75: (1)-(2)

(1) A public authority shall in carrying out its functions relating to Northern Ireland have due regard to the need to promote equality of opportunity:

    (a) between persons of different religious belief, political opinion, racial group, age, marital status or sexual orientation;

    (b) between men and women generally;

    (c) between persons with a disability and persons without; and

    (d) between persons with dependants and persons without.

(2) Without prejudice to its obligations under subsection (1), a public authority shall in carrying out its functions relating to Northern Ireland have regard to the desirability of promoting good relations between persons of different religious belief, political opinion or racial group.

Section 76: (1)

(1) It shall be unlawful for a public authority carrying out functions relating to Northern Ireland to discriminate, or to aid or incite another person to discriminate, against a person or class of person on the ground of religious belief or political opinion.

4
Fair Employment and Treatment (Northern Ireland) Order
(1998)

Section 2: (3)

(3) In this Order references to a person's religious belief or political opinion include references to:

(a) his supposed religious belief or political opinion; and

(b) the absence or supposed absence of any, or any particular, religious belief or political opinion.

Section 3: (1), (2), (3)

(1) In this Order 'discrimination' means:

(a) discrimination on the ground of religious belief or political opinion; or

(b) discrimination by way of victimisation;

and 'discriminate' shall be construed accordingly.

(2) A person discriminates against another person on the ground of religious belief or political opinion in any circumstances relevant for the purposes of this Order if:

(a) on either of those grounds he treats that other less favourably than he treats or would treat other persons; or

(b) he applies to that other a requirement or condition which he applies or would apply equally to persons not of the same religious belief or political opinion as that other but:

   (i) which is such that the proportion of persons of the same religious belief or of the same political opinion as that other who can comply with it is considerably smaller than the proportion of persons not of that religious belief or, as the case requires, not of that political opinion who can comply with it; and

   (ii) which he cannot show to be justifiable irrespective of the religious belief or political opinion of the person to whom it is applied; and

   (iii) which is to the detriment of that other because he cannot comply with it.

(3) A comparison of the cases of persons of different religious belief or political opinion under paragraph (2) must be such that the relevant circumstances in the one case are the same, or not materially different, in the other.

5
[Republic of Ireland] **Employment Equality Act** (1998)

Section 6: (1), (2)

(1) For the purposes of this Act, discrimination shall be taken to occur where, on any of the grounds in subsection (2) (in this Act referred to as 'the discriminatory grounds'), one person is treated less favourably than another is, has been or would be treated.

(2) As between any 2 persons, the discriminatory grounds (and the descriptions of those grounds for the purposes of this Act) are:

   (a) that one is a woman and the other is a man (in this Act referred to as 'the gender ground'),

   (b) that they are of different marital status (in this Act referred to as 'the marital status ground'),

   (c) that one has family status and the other does not (in this Act referred to as 'the family status ground'),

   (d) that they are of different sexual orientation (in this Act referred to as 'the sexual orientation ground'),

   (e) that one has a different religious belief from the other, or that one has a religious belief and the other has not (in this Act referred to as 'the religion ground'),

   (f) that they are of different ages, but subject to subsection (3) (in this Act referred to as 'the age ground'),

   (g) that one is a person with a disability and the other either is not or is a person with a different disability (in this Act referred to as 'the disability ground'),

   (h) that they are of different race, colour, nationality or ethnic or national origins (in this Act referred to as 'the ground of race'),

   (i) that one is a member of the traveller community and the other is not (in this Act referred to as 'the traveller community ground').

Section 37: (1)

(1) A religious, educational or medical institution which is under the direction or control of a body established for religious purposes or whose objectives include the provision of services in an environment which

promotes certain religious values shall not be taken to discriminate against a person for the purposes of this Part or Part II if:

(a) it gives more favourable treatment, on the religion ground, to an employee or a prospective employee over that person where it is reasonable to do so in order to maintain the religious ethos of the institution; or

(b) it takes action which is reasonably necessary to prevent an employee or a prospective employee from undermining the religious ethos of the institution.

6
[Republic of Ireland] Equal Status Act (2000)

Section 7: (2), (3)(a)–(c)

(2) An educational establishment shall not discriminate in relation to:

(a) the admission or the terms or conditions of admission of a person as a student to the establishment;

(b) the access of a student to any course, facility or benefit provided by the establishment;

(c) any other term or condition of participation in the establishment by a student; or

(d) the expulsion of a student from the establishment or any other sanction against the student.

(3) An educational establishment does not discriminate under subsection (2) by reason only that:

(a) where the establishment is not a third-level institution and admits students of one gender only, it refuses to admit as a student a person who is not of that gender;

(b) where the establishment is an institution established for the purpose of providing training to ministers of religion and admits students of only one gender or religious belief, it refuses to admit as a student a person who is not of that gender or religious belief;

(c) where the establishment is a school providing primary or post-primary education to students and the objective of the school is to provide education in an environment which promotes certain religious values, it admits persons of a particular religious denomination in preference to others or it refuses to admit as a student a person who is not of that denomination and, in the case of a refusal, it is proved that the refusal is essential to maintain the ethos of the school.

7
EU Employment Directive (2000)

Article 1

The purpose of this Directive is to lay down a general framework for combating discrimination on the grounds of religion or belief, disability, age or sexual orientation as regards employment and occupation, with a view to putting into effect in the Member States the principle of equal treatment.

Article 4

(1) Member States may provide that a difference of treatment which is based on a characteristic related to any of the grounds referred to in Article 1 shall not constitute discrimination where, by reason of the nature of the particular occupational activities concerned or of the context in which they are carried out, such a characteristic constitutes a genuine and determining occupational requirement, provided that the objective is legitimate and the requirement is proportionate.

(2) Member States may maintain national legislation in force at the date of adoption of this Directive or provide for future legislation incorporating national practices existing at the date of adoption of this Directive pursuant to which, in the case of occupational activities within churches and other public or private organisations the ethos of which is based on religion or belief, a difference of treatment based on a person's religion or belief shall not constitute discrimination where, by reason of the nature of these activities or of the context in which they are carried out, a person's religion or belief constitute a genuine, legitimate and justified occupational requirement, having regard to the organisation's ethos. This difference of treatment shall be implemented taking account of Member States' constitutional provisions and principles, as well as the general principles of Community law, and should not justify discrimination on another ground.

Provided that its provisions are otherwise complied with, this Directive shall thus not prejudice the right of churches and other public or private organisations, the ethos of which is based on religion or belief, acting in conformity with national constitutions and laws, to require individuals working for them to act in good faith and with loyalty to the organisation's ethos.

Closed and open views of the Other

Distinctions	Closed views of the Other	Open views of the Other
1. *Monolithic / diverse*	The Other seen as a single monolithic bloc, static and unresponsive to new realities	The Other seen as diverse and progressive, with internal differences, debates and development
2. *Separate / interacting*	The Other seen as separate: (a) not having any aims or values in common with the self; (b) not affected by it; (c) not influencing it	The Other seen as interdependent with the self: (a) having certain shared values and aims; (b) affected by it; (c) enriching it
3. *Inferior / different*	The Other seen as inferior to the self: e.g. barbaric, irrational, 'fundamentalist'	The Other seen as different but of equal worth
4. *Enemy / partner*	The Other seen as violent, aggressive, threatening, to be defeated and perhaps dominated	The Other seen as an actual or potential partner in joint co-operative enterprises and in the solution of shared problems
5. *Manipulative / sincere*	The Other seen as manipulative and deceitful, bent only on material or strategic advantage	The Other seen as sincere in their beliefs, not hypocritical
6. *Criticism of the self rejected / considered*	Criticisms made by the Other of the self are rejected out of hand	Criticisms of the self are considered and debated
7. *Discrimination defended / criticised*	Hostility towards the Other used to justify discriminatory practices and exclusion of the Other from mainstream society	Debates and disagreements with the Other do not diminish efforts to combat discrimination and exclusion
8. *Hostility towards the Other seen as natural / problematic*	Fear and hostility towards the Other accepted as natural and 'normal'	Critical views of the Other themselves subjected to critique, lest they be inaccurate and unfair

This table is taken from *The Future of Multi-Ethnic Britain: The Parekh Report* (London: Profile Books, 2000), p. reproduced by kind permission of The Runnymede Trust's Commission on the Future of Multi-Ethnic Britain.

Notes

Asking some questions

1. Paul Weller, Alice Feldman, Kingsley Purdam, et al., *Religious Discrimination in England and Wales*, London, Home Office Research Study 220, 2001, p. 116.

2. Weller, Feldman, Purdam et al., *Religious Discrimination*, pp. 103f., mentioning in particular Muslims and Christians in black-led Churches; to some extent Sikhs and Hindus; also Mormons, Jehovah's Witnesses and members of some New Religious Movements.

3. Both the Republic of Ireland and Northern Ireland already have legal provisions against religious discrimination – cf. Appendix One (3)–(6).

1 The meaning of religious discrimination

1. This is apparent in one of the most commonly cited definitive legal comments on the characteristics of religion, that of Mr Justice Dillon in *Re South Place Ethical Society: Barralet v A-G* (1980): 'It seems to me that two of the essential attributes of religion are faith and worship; faith in god and worship of that god.' The judge went on to admit: 'It is said that religion cannot be necessarily theist or dependent on belief in a god, a supernatural or supreme being, because Buddhism does not have any such belief. I do not think it is necessary to explore that further in this judgement because I do not know enough about Buddhism. It may be that the answer in respect of Buddhism is to treat it as an exception ... Alternatively, it may be that Buddhism is not an exception ...' cited in S. H. Bailey, D. J. Harris and B. L. Jones (eds), *Civil Liberties: Cases and Materials*, London, Butterworth, 4th ed., 1995, pp. 579f.

2. Recognition of this problem with respect to Buddhism goes back at least as far as Durkheim. However, there are also other problematical cases. For example, Jainism can be viewed in different senses as 'atheist in the

43

limited sense of a rejection of both the existence of a creator god and the possibility of the intervention of such a being in human affairs', and at the same time as 'a theist religion in the more profound sense that it accepts the existence of a divine principle' – Paul Dundas, *The Jains*, London, Routledge, 1992, p. 94. In the case of both Jainism and Buddhism, it seems that categorization as either 'atheism' or 'theism' is basically inappropriate.

3. For example, those religious traditions with national faith organizations in membership of the Inter Faith Network for the UK: Baha'i, Buddhist, Christian, Hindu, Jain, Jewish, Muslim, Sikh and Zoroastrian.

4. *Kokkinakis v Greece* (1993), cited in D. J. Harris, M. O'Boyle and C. Warbrick, *Law of the European Convention of Human Rights*, London, Butterworth, 1995, p. 357.

5. On the relation in legal contexts between 'religion', 'belief' and 'religious belief', see further below, n. 16 of chapter 4.

6. Paul Weller and Kingsley Purdam (eds), *Religious Discrimination in England and Wales: Interim Report*, Derby, University of Derby, 2000, p. 8.

7. Weller and Purdam (eds), *Interim Report*, p. 10.

8. Weller and Purdam (eds), *Interim Report*, p. 9.

2 Christians and religious freedom

1. This was the formula used at the Peace of Augsburg (1555) by which the princes of the Empire settled whether their own lands should be Roman Catholic or Lutheran.

2. *The Mistery of Iniquity* (1612), cited in Nigel Wright, *Public Truth or Private Option? Gospel and Religious Liberty in a Multi-Faith Society in the Light of the Resurrection*, Joppa Group Occasional Paper, 1999.

3. *Syllabus Pii IX, seu Collectio errorum in diversis Actis Pii IX proscriptorum* (1864), Nos. 2978–2979, in H. Denzinger and A. Schönmetzer, *Enchiridion Symbolorum Definitionum et Declarationum de Rebus Fidei et Morum*, Barcelona, Herder, 36th ed., 1975.

4. *Dignitatis Humanae* 2, in Austin Flannery, OP, *Vatican Council II: The Conciliar and Post-Conciliar Documents*, Dublin, Dominican Publications, 1975.

5. The extent of reinterpretation is cited by Gavin D'Costa as evidence of a clear development in official Roman Catholic teaching – *The Meeting of Religions and the Trinity*, Maryknoll, Orbis, 2000, pp. 134ff. D'Costa notes that John Courtney Murray, SJ, who was largely responsible for drafting the successive texts of *Dignitatis Humanae*, felt that much of the opposition to the declaration arose from a perception that it called into question the irreversibility of magisterial pronouncements.

6. *Catechism of the Catholic Church*, London, Geoffrey Chapman, 1994, §2108.

7. The ECHR speaks of manifestation in terms of 'worship, teaching, practice and observance', Article 9 (1) – see Appendix One (1). It is clearly not possible always to distinguish sharply between these various types of activity. It has been established that 'practice' is not so broad as to cover 'each act which is motivated or influenced by a religion or belief' – *Arrowsmith v UK* (1978), cf. Harris, O'Boyle and Warbrick, *Law*, p. 363.

8. *Dignitatis Humanae* 3, in Flannery, *Documents*.

9. Matthew 11.28-30. Cf. also the numerous occasions in the Gospels where Jesus allows space for his hearers to reject his message, notably John 6.66-68, where this option is explicitly made available to the inner core of the twelve apostles.

10. John 18.36-37. It is in this sense also that Matthew 22.21 ('Render to Caesar the things that are Caesar's, and to God the things that are God's') should be understood.

11. E.g. Acts 3.17-26; 1 Corinthians 2.3-5.

12. 'Conversion' here is used in the primary sense of a person's decision to change religious allegiance, rather than in the secondary (transitive) sense of another person seeking to persuade them to make such a decision. The latter also raises complex and sensitive issues in a multi-faith situation. A helpful preliminary discussion is to be found in a paper prepared by the Inter Faith Network for the UK, *Mission, Dialogue and Inter Religious Encounter: A Consultative Document*, London, IFN, 1993. However, there is a need for more detailed work on the appropriateness, in concrete terms, of particular forms of missionary activity in a religiously plural society.

13. This is one in the list of the permissible limitations on manifestation listed in general terms in Article 9 (2) of ECHR – see Appendix One (1).

14. See, e.g., Carolyn Evans, *Freedom of Religion under the European Convention on Human Rights*, Oxford, OUP, 2001.

15. So, for example, unlike the ECHR, worldwide human rights documents since the *Universal Declaration of Human Rights* (1948) have not referred unambiguously to 'freedom to change religion', because of opposition from some Islamic states. The *International Covenant on Civil and Political Rights* (1976) spoke merely of 'freedom to have or adopt a religion', though the UN's Human Rights Committee maintained ('General Comment', July 1993) that this 'necessarily entails ... the right to replace one's current religion or belief with another' – see Kevin Boyle and Juliet Sheen (eds), *Freedom of Religion and Belief: A World Report*, London, Routledge, 1997.

3 The Churches and religious discrimination

1. In 2000, CCRJ's Ecumenical Racial Justice Fund dispensed approximately £300,000 to over 100 projects in Britain and Ireland combating racism through empowering black and ethnic minority people.

2. Weller, Feldman and Purdam, et al., *Religious Discrimination*, p. 12. A similar overlap of religious and racial identity, and consequent experience of double discrimination, can be found among Rastafarians. See William Spencer, *Dread Jesus*, London, SPCK, 1999, for a detailed discussion of the relation between Rastafarianism and Christianity.

3. Weller and Purdam (eds), *Interim Report*, p. 15.

4. *Mandla v. Dowell Lee* (1983), cited in Bailey, Harris and Jones, *Civil Liberties*, p. 639.

5. Iqbal Sacranie, 'Welcome Speech by Secretary General Muslim Council of Britain, at a Muslim reception in honour of The Rt Hon Tony Blair, Prime Minister, London, 5 May 1999', on Muslim Council of Britain website, http://www.mcb.org.uk.

6. Commission on British Muslims and Islamophobia: *Islamophobia – a challenge to us all*, London, Runnymede Trust, 1997, recommendations 47, 48, 50 (p. 64).

7. Report of the Commission chaired by Lord (Bhikhu) Parekh, *The Future of Multi-Ethnic Britain*, London, Profile, 2000, p. 247. Eight differences between 'open' and 'closed' views are elaborated in Table 17.1, reproduced as Appendix Two of this report by kind permission of the Commission.

8. Cf. Inter Faith Consultative Group of the Archbishops' Council, *Sharing One Hope? The Church of England and Christian–Jewish Relations: A Contribution to a Continuing Debate*, London, Church House Publishing, 2001.

9. John Paul II, *Incarnationis Mysterium* (1998), §11, cited in Vatican International Theological Commission, *Memory and Reconciliation: The Church and the Faults of the Past*, Rome, Congregation for the Doctrine of the Faith, 1999, which carefully discusses the theological issues involved in this approach.

10. *Building Good Relations with People of Different Faiths and Beliefs*, London, IFN, 1993. The whole of this short statement is exceptionally valuable in spelling out the implications of such dialogue, and has added authority because it was prepared and endorsed by a wide range of organizations with an interest in inter faith relations, including national representative bodies of all the major faiths in the UK.

11. Cf. CCIFR, *Problem or Opportunity? Christians and Local Inter Faith Activity*, London, CTBI, 2000, which includes practical suggestions for Christians wishing to develop an inter faith involvement.

12. This expression has been current in anti-discrimination legislation (Sex Discrimination and Race Relations Acts) for many years, and is also used to define exemptions in the *EU Employment Directive (2000)* – cf. Appendix One (7).

13. For a detailed discussion of a particular issue of this kind as faced by one Church, cf. the report of the Inter Faith Consultative Group of the Church of England, *Communities and Buildings – Church of England Premises and Other Faiths*, London, Church House Publishing, 1996.

4 The law and religious discrimination

1. A report by the Law Commission observed of other Christian Churches that: 'It seems probable that at most other denominations are protected only to the extent that their fundamental beliefs are those which are held in common with the established Church', *Criminal Law: Offences against Religion and Public Worship* – Law Commission Report No. 79, 1981, p. 82 para 6.9.

2. *Ex p Choudhury*, 1991.

3. E.g. Shabbir Akhtar describes this as a 'particularly obvious inequality within the law'. 'Holy Freedom and the "Liberals"', p. 254, in M. M. Ahsan and A. R. Kidwai (eds), *Sacrilege versus Civility: Muslim Perspectives on* The Satanic Verses *Affair*, Leicester, Islamic Foundation, 1991, pp. 251–260.

4. Abolition without replacement was called for in a second report from the Law Commission entitled *Criminal Law: Offences against Religion and Public Worship* – Law Commission Report No. 145, 1985. An Archbishop of Canterbury's Working Group chaired by the Bishop of London in 1989 recommended the extension of the offence to other religions also.

5. Religious belief is one of the grounds on which discrimination is prohibited in the area of employment by the *Employment Equality Act 1998*, and in the provision of goods, services and facilities by the *Equal Status Act 2000*. Both laws include exemptions allowing for discrimination in various contexts by religious bodies or bodies related to religious belief in various ways. Cf. Appendix One (5), (6).

6. The *Northern Ireland Act 1998* prohibits discrimination on the grounds of religion or belief by government and public bodies, and the *Fair Employment and Treatment (Northern Ireland) Order 1998* prohibits discrimination in employment, requiring employers with more than ten full-time employees to register with the Equality Commission. Texts in Appendix One (3), (4).

7. See page 19 for the limited and indirect provision available under the *Race Relations Act 1976*.

8. See texts, Appendix One (2), (7).

9. Cf. Appendix One (1). The ECHR rights include freedom to change religion and freedom to manifest religion.

10. Such a general prohibition of discrimination on grounds of (*inter alia*) religion in 'the enjoyment of any right set forth by law' is set out in a proposed 'Protocol No. 12' to the ECHR that has been signed by a number of member states of the Council of Europe. The Republic of Ireland is among the signatories, but the UK Government has declined to sign.

11. This 'Employment Directive' (2000/78/EC) under Article 13 of the EU Treaty followed a 'Race Directive' (2000/43/EC) under the same Article, which extended the prohibition on racial discrimination to include also areas such as the provision of goods and services.

12. Text in Appendix One (7).

13. Thirty-three key issues of this kind are identified and discussed in the extremely lucid paper commissioned by the Home Office from the Centre for Public Law at Cambridge: Bob Hepple and Tufyal Choudhury, *Tackling Religious Discrimination: Practical Implications for Policy-Makers and Legislators*, London, Home Office Research Study 221, 2001.

14. The principal case here is the judgement on the South Place Ethical Society, *Barralet v A-G* (1980) – cf. Chapter 1, n. 1 (p. 43 above). A similar approach in *Ex p Segerdal* (1970) had led the Court of Appeal to conclude that Scientology was *not* a religion, but in *Church of the New Faith v Comr for Pay-roll Tax* (1983) it was held that Scientology *was* a religion so as to attract tax-exemption. The Charity Commissioners in a review of case law – with specific reference to the status of Scientology – concluded in 1999 that the 'English authorities were neither clear nor unambiguous as to the definition of religion in English Charity law' (cited in Hepple and Choudhury, *Tackling Religious Discrimination*, p. 28, para 4.7).

15. See Appendix One (3)-(6), for the Irish provisions. Other examples include Canada (at the federal and various provincial levels), several Australian states, New Zealand, USA (*Civil Rights Act 1964*), and the Netherlands – cf. Hepple and Choudhury, *Tackling Religious Discrimination*, Appendix 1, pp. 67ff.

16. Religious belief in the Northern Ireland legislation (*Fair Employment and Treatment Order*, Article 2 (3)) is specifically defined in the way we are following here, to embrace 'the absence ... of any, or any particular, religious beliefs'. Carolyn Evans, *Freedom of Religion*, includes a careful discussion of the issues involved in interpreting the ECHR (Article 9) assertion of freedom to 'manifest' belief with reference to the Arrowsmith case (*Arrowsmith v UK*, 1978), which concerned the limits that could be set by the state within a military setting of the individual's right to propagate the ideology of pacifism.

17. The exemptions also formed a particular focus in the scrutiny of the draft directive by the House of Lords Select Committee on the European Union, and Churches and other faith communities contributed significantly to those discussions.

18. See Appendix One (7). Article 4 (2), which was designed to ensure that the existing employment policies of religious organizations were not pressurized to change as a result of new legislation, is permissive in the sense that member states may take advantage of it but need not do so.

19. The question of appropriate exemptions to safeguard the integrity of religious organizations was also intensively addressed by the UK Churches in relation to the drafting of the Human Rights Act. As a result, Section 13 of that Act emphasizes the need for 'particular regard to the importance' of freedom of religion in such contexts – see text, Appendix One (2).

20. The idea of 'reasonable accommodation' has achieved prominence in UK anti-discrimination legislation through the *Disability Discrimination Act*, which lays down 'a primary duty to make reasonable adjustments where arrangements or physical features of premises place a disabled person at a substantial disadvantage compared with persons who are not disabled' – summary in Hepple and Choudhury, *Tackling Religious Discrimination*, p. 37, para 6.8.

Index

Related titles from Churches Together in Britain and Ireland

Christian Mission in Western Society

This stimulating collection of essays from a variety of contributors creatively and provocatively explores the past, present and future of Christianity in the west and the challenges facing Churches in an increasingly fragmented, postmodern and apparently secular world.

£11.50   0 85169 246 X

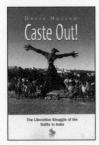

Caste Out: The Liberation Struggle of the Dalits in India

This book by David Haslam is the result of his sabbatical journey to India and Pakistan. He provides a sympathetic outsider's glimpse of India's caste system and the liberation struggle of the Dalits. He draws a comparison between casteism and racism and calls upon the Church to play its part in overcoming caste oppression across India.

£4.95   0 85169 250 8

Wrestling and Resting

Wrestling and Resting is an exploration of the spirituality of Britain and Ireland through a series of moving and funny stories, commentary and poems by authors including Jim Cotter, Jan Berry and Ruth Burgess. The stories are rooted in people's local situations and offer a patchwork picture of spirituality today.

£13.95   0 85169 248 6

All titles are available from Church House Bookshop
Telephone orders: 020 7898 1300/02
Order securely online: www.chbookshop.co.uk

Christians and Jews: A New Way of Thinking

This booklet is written for British Christians in the hope that through it they may find a new way of thinking about the Jewish faith and Jewish people. It sets out where British and Irish Churches now stand in the continuing process of exploration and reflection. It also enables serious thought to be given to why antisemitism persists and how it can be rooted out.

£1.50   **Only available from CTBI. To order contact 020 7523 2121**